Friends

Friends

Japanese and Tennesseans

A Model of U.S. – Japan Cooperation

Governor Lamar Alexander

Photographs by Robin Hood

Kodansha International Ltd. Tokyo, New York and San Francisco

Design by Ann Harakawa.

Distributed in the United States by Kodansha International/
USA Ltd., through Harper & Row, Publishers, Inc., 10 East 53rd
Street, New York, New York 10022.

Published by Kodansha International Ltd., 12–21, Otowa
2-chome, Bunkyo-ku, Tokyo 112 and Kodansha International/
USA Ltd., with offices at 10 East 53rd Street, New York, New
York 10022 and The Hearst Building, 5 Third Street, Suite 430,
San Francisco, California 94103.

Printed in Japan.
FIRST EDITION, 1986.

Library of Congress Cataloging-in-Publication Data
Alexander, Lamar
   Friends, Japanese and Tennesseans.

   1. United States—Relations—Japan—Pictorial works.
2. Japan—Relations—United States—Pictorial works.
3. Tennessee—Relations—Japan—Pictorial works.
4. Japan—Relations—Tennessee—Pictorial works.
5. Japan—Description and travel—1945—Views.
6. Tennessee—Description and travel—1981—Views.
I. Title.
E183.8.J3A44   1986   976.8′004956   85–45733

ISBN 0–87011–759–9 (U.S.)
ISBN 4–7700–1259–4 (in Japan)

For Mike Mansfield, a good teacher

Contents

Preface   13

Introduction   15

1 At Home in the Mountains: The Land   25

2 The Match Game: Customs and Lifestyles   71

3 Japan Comes to Tennessee   149

4 A Bridge to the Sun   173

This book tells the story, in words and pictures, of the extraordinary friendship developing between a Pacific island nation and an inland American state—each generally seen from a single, often stereotypical, viewpoint by the other.

The book is a gift to the businesses and people of Japan who have made Tennessee their home away from home. It comes from Tennesseans who are grateful for the $1.2 billion in new investment, the thousands of new jobs, and, especially, the new friendships that the thirty-two Japanese businesses in our state (at last count) have produced.

The book is also for the people of Tennessee. I hope it helps Tennesseans to understand how much our relationship with Japan can help us as America enters the Century of the Pacific. And finally, this book is for any American or Japanese citizen who, even at this moment when trade arguments sour the relations between our two countries, is ready to enjoy the story of how a friendship can grow between our two peoples.

The idea for the book came from the fertile mind of Tennessee's Pulitzer Prize-winning photographer with the improbable name, Robin Hood. He spent five months in Japan and more time than that in Tennessee capturing differences and similarities on film. Kodansha, Japan's largest publisher, accepted the book to help people on both sides of the Pacific better understand each other *and* the most important two-country relationship in the world.

I would like to thank four Tennessee banking companies that have helped to build the bridge from Tennessee to Japan, for underwriting the costs of photography: Commerce Union Corporation, First American Corporation, First Tennessee, and Third National Bank, an affiliate of Third National Corporation. To help keep the price of the book down, I have contributed the text, gratis.

Tad Akaishi, a Presbyterian seminary student in Japan during World War II who now runs Kodansha's U.S. operations from New York, produced the book. Ann Harakawa designed it. Doug LaFrenier edited it. Marc Lavine's research, the patience of Ed Liden and the support of Tom Ingram, and the typing of Faye Forehand, Wendy Douglas, and Roxann Ghee made it happen. It was fun to work with them all.

Lamar Alexander

Lamar Alexander
Nashville

Introduction

Tokyo, November 3, 1979: "Don't discuss the War." That's the Supreme Command, the one thing an American Governor seeking Japanese investment does *not* do. Our state economic development officials were sure of that. They had learned it trudging into thirty-eight Tokyo boardrooms during the last five days. Tonight their feet hurt. They surrounded me at Narita airport, determined to tell me, before I began my calls, what their mistakes had taught them:

• Never arrive late. It may be fashionable at home but it is disrespectful here.

• Always shake hands first with the Number One Man when several Japanese businessmen enter the room. He is almost always the oldest, sometimes in his seventies. Don't hug him as if he were your long-lost Uncle Joe. Japanese don't touch, and they are uncomfortable with Americans who do.

• Don't look at the interpreter. Look at your Japanese host, even while the interpreter translates. You'll get used to it. (I never have.)

• Don't just thank them for their gift. Unwrap it. Admire it. If you don't know what it is, ask. And don't forget to give your gift in return.

• Don't sip the green tea. Slurp it. Hold the bowl with both hands and sluurrpp it, often and with enthusiasm. And for heaven's sake, don't demand a Coke.

• Stay awake during the fifteen-course evening meal even if you suddenly remember that in Nashville it is 5:00 a.m. If your legs cramp because you're sitting cross-legged on the floor, go to the bathroom and stretch. And eat the raw tuna, even if its head still wriggles. They've eaten raw fish for centuries, and they're healthier than we are.

• Don't leave a tip. They will think you forgot your money and chase you across town to return it.

By early 1985, ten pecent or $1.2 billion of all Japanese investment in the fifty United States was in one state: Tennessee. We had learned our Japanese manners.

But then, in 1979, I was a new student, trying to avoid the wrong things and even to do a right thing or two. The President of the United States, Jimmy Carter, had said, "Governors: go to Japan. Persuade them to make in the United States what they sell in the United States. Bring their plants and those jobs to your states. And while you're there, persuade those Japanese to buy more of what we sell." The U.S. trade deficit with Japan, even though the American dollar was weak then, had become embarrassing to both countries. Americans were buying, driving, sitting on, playing with, and watching Japanese products. The President meant for us to help him do something about it.

As late as 1975, Sumitomo Chemical in Mount Pleasant had been the only Japanese plant in Tennessee, and fewer than fifteen hundred Japanese lived among our state's population of four million. In the Great Japanese Plant Hunt, we were rookies and our neighboring states were our toughest competitors. Take Georgia. The Saturday night in 1979 when I arrived in Tokyo, sixty Japanese companies located in Georgia held a Tokyo reception in honor of the Governor of Georgia. *They* were honoring *him* while I was practicing my new manners. By Monday, three hundred industrial recruiters and business leaders from seven states would arrive for the fourth annual meeting of the Southeast United States/Japan Association, a group designed to push Japanese plants into the American southeast and American exports into Japan. Twenty-three states had sent plant-hunting delegations to Japan during 1979; twenty-eight were already signed up for 1980.

So there I was in Japan, 7,500 miles from my home in the Great Smoky Mountains of East Tennessee. When I had campaigned for Governor only one year earlier, not one Tennessean had said to me,

"When you're elected, go to Japan." Tennesseans wanted better jobs, but getting them from Japan was not on their minds. And my own idea of Japan then was a picture-postcard stereotype: hot springs, Mt. Fuji, and Madame Butterfly, somewhere on the other side of the world.

That first Saturday evening at Narita airport, my wife Honey and I found a taxi. I handed the driver a note in Japanese characters explaining that we wanted to go the Imperial Hotel. "Americans?" the driver asked. "Yes," I replied, offering a calling card with my name in English on one side, in Japanese on the other.

The taxi moved away from the airport to the brightly lit expressway to Tokyo. "Imperial Hotel was not bombed. Neither was Emperor's Palace. Same Emperor since before War," the driver said. "Almost everything else bombed. Wooden buildings. Terrible fire bombs. City is rebuilt. Now twelve million people. Too many." He laughed the little laugh that punctuates most Japanese-American conversations. The taxi sped into the center of the city. His story rushed ahead: "I was in Japanese navy. Stationed in Pacific. Saw many American bombers...." So much, I thought, for the Supreme Command, for not discussing the War.

Small cars and tiny vans waited patiently, bumper-to-bumper, at stoplights. Most switched off their headlights—some stopped their engines—until the green lights flashed. "Saving energy," explained the driver. "In Japan no oil, no coal. We buy energy from other countries." The shadows along the streets of the old capital city obscured an irregular assortment of anonymous gray buildings, not one a skyscraper, all completed since 1945. I had not realized that the firebombing of Tokyo had caused more destruction, more loss of life, than the atomic bombing of Hiroshima and Nagasaki.

Since 1979, I have traveled to Japan eight times, visited four times with the Prime Minister of Japan, and met dozens of times with ambassadors, government leaders and business officials. In all of my meetings, I notice how the War lingers, especially on our side, helping to spoil America's alliance with Japan. So many Americans remember the brutal death marches from Japanese prison camps in China, so many Japanese remember seeing American bomber pilots' faces as they flew low, spreading fire over Tokyo, that some forget that the War is over and that most of the biggest players have switched sides. Most Americans undersand that Russia, our ally in the war, is now our No. 1 adversary. But it seems harder for us to imagine that Japan, once our enemy, is now our No. 1 ally.

Our Ambassador to Japan, Mike Mansfield, a Marine who fought in World Wars I and II, says in every speech that "the Japan-American alliance is the most important two-country relationship in the world, *bar none*." He says this so often and so passionately that Americans in Tokyo jokingly refer to our embassy there as "The Bar None Ranch."

I agree with Ambassador Mansfield. I have now seen first-hand how Japan has become Tennessee's port-of-entry to the nations of the Pacific Rim, where *sixty percent* of the world's people live. In my own state, I have seen how many new weekly paychecks can be generated when businessmen work together from the two countries that produce one-third of all the world's dollars and trade, and one-half of the world's foreign investment and bank loans. And after flying uncomfortably near the spot where the Soviets shot down Korean Air Line 007 on its way to Tokyo, I understand better how important it is for our 7th Fleet to have free bases in Japan.

Since my first taxi ride into Tokyo in 1979, Tennessee has become the new American "home away from home" for Japanese business. Perhaps our story can help strengthen the new bridges being built from America to the Land of the Rising Sun. Tennesseans and our Japanese friends have reached beyond our bitter war memories and our other profound differences by the simplest of devices: we have gotten to know one another.

Robin Hood's photographs show the joy we have had finding familiar glimpses of our own life deep within Japanese culture. In Chapter I, they reveal how much alike are our mountains, our seasons, and our landscapes. Did you know that Tokyo and Nashville and Knoxville are all on the same latitude? That makes our climates similar.

Chapter II finds similar strains in our vastly different heritages: compare the country pagodas and country churches, tobacco harvests in each place, the guitar player at Ueno Park outside Tokyo and Levi Collins in the Cumberland Mountains.

Chapter III is the remarkable story of how ten percent of Japan's U.S. investment found its way to Tennessee.

And Chapter IV describes how, despite our official differences, our common needs inevitably suggest a future of friendship between our countries and peoples.

We have found that knowing our Japanese friends not only brings us better jobs and more money, it makes our lives richer. The Japanese have learned a lot about us, too. During my 1979 visit, I found that, if they knew anything about Tennessee at all, it was Brenda Lee, the Tennessee Waltz, and Jack Daniel's. That first evening at the airport, Jim

Cotham, our economic development chief, gave me a lesson about what to expect.

"Take a map," Jim urged.

"Of Tokyo?" I asked.

"Of the United States."

"Why the United States?"

"Because," explained Jim, "at the end of my seventh visit, after I had made my best pitch, my Japanese business prospect smiled politely and, through his interpreter, said:

"'Thank you, Mr. Cot-ham.

"'Now, please tell me, just what *is* a Tennessee?'"

Lebanon

Lavergne

Smyrna

Nashville

Shelbyville

Lewisburg

Fayetteville

Tennessee

The table indicates the sites of 32 Japanese firms that have located in Tennessee since 1975, accounting for some $1.2 billion in investment and providing jobs for nearly 8,000 Tennesseans.

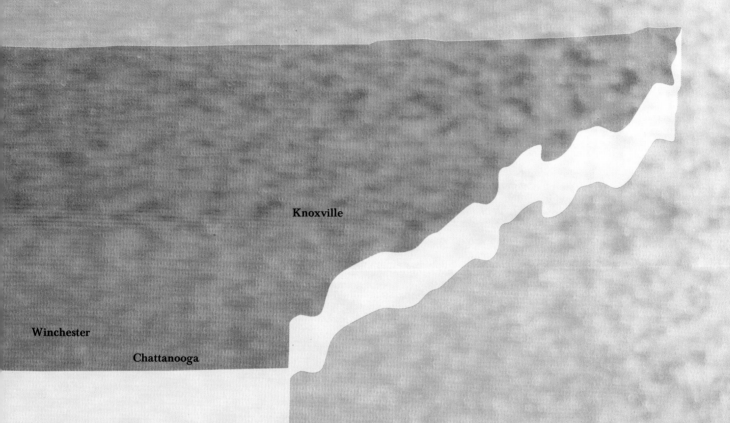

Memphis
Goh Shoji Company, Inc.
Gulf Coast Grain, Inc.
Mitsui and Company (U.S.A.)
Mitsui Grain Corporation
NKC of America, Inc.
Nisco Steel Services, Inc.
Nissan Industrial Equipment Company
Sharp Manufacturing Company of America
Toshiba Medical Systems

Jackson
Tabuchi Electric Company of America

Nashville
Chuetsu Metal, U.S.A., Inc.
Clarion Corporation of America
Kagiya Trading Company Limited of America
Kohl-Madden Printing Ink Corporation
Marubeni America Corporation
Nissan Fire and Marine Insurance Company, Limited
Nissan Trading Corporation, U.S.A.
Pearl International, Inc.
Polychrome Corporation
Tsubakimoto Engineering of America, Inc.
Yasuda Fire and Marine Insurance Company
YKK USA, Inc.

Lebanon
Toshiba America Inc.

Lavergne
Bridgestone Tire Manufacturing (U.S.A.), Inc.

Smyrna
Nissan Motor Corporation in U.S.A.
Nissan Motor Manufacturing Corporation U.S.A.

Shelbyville
Calsonic Manufacturing Corporation

Lewisburg
Kantus Corporation

Fayetteville
Tennessee Fan Company

Knoxville
Matsushita Electronic Components Company

Chattanooga
Komatsu America Manufacturing Corporation

Winchester
CKR Industries, Inc.

Fukuoka

Nagasaki

Kumamoto

Shikok

Kyushu

Hokkaido

Japan

The Japanese archipelago has
a land mass about three and a half
times the size of Tennessee and
a population of nearly 120 million
people. Tokyo is on the same latitude
as Nashville, Tennessee.

Morioka

Honshu

Nikko

Takayama

Kyoto
Nara
Kamakura
Tokyo

1

At Home in the Mountains: The Land

Spin Tennessee on an imaginary pinwheel and let Bristol touch Cincinnati, Ohio, while Memphis touches Montgomery, Alabama. That is about the position of Japan: same latitude as ours, other side of the world. That is why our mountains, our climate, our seasons, and our love of nature are so much alike.

Before I saw Nikko, I didn't realize what it meant for Tokyo and Nashville to be on the same latitude.

Nikko is a lovely town of shrines and temples about seventy-five miles north of Tokyo. It reminded me of Gatlinburg, nestled in mountains that are as much like the Great Smoky Mountains as we Tennesseans are likely to find anywhere in the world.

It was my first trip to Japan, in 1979. Our pilgrimage from Tennessee had begun on a cold November Friday. Flying west from Chicago, our plane had chased the sun across the sky for fifteen consecutive daylight hours. It was late Saturday when we saw Japan; Friday night vanished somewhere during the chase across the international dateline. (Today in Tennessee is almost always tomorrow in Japan.) As the plane dropped through thickening clouds, a ragged row of islands emerged. Mountains rose to meet us, then disappeared in the clouds. They descended almost to the coasts, as mountains do in Monterey, California, and Valparaiso, Chile. This was Japan, the Land of the Rising Sun, an archipelago of islands created one-by-one by the frolicking gods—so the legends go—and ruled today by an Emperor whose distant forefather purportedly descended from those same gods.

After too little sleep in Tokyo, we took an express train to Nikko on Sunday, our first morning in Japan. My eyelids were as heavy as sandbags. But I'll never forget the sight of Nikko. The priest Shodo, who founded the first temple there in 782, compared it to Buddha's "pure land." Travelers there have learned from the Japanese: "Never say magnificent until you've seen Nikko."

Except for the Buddhist temples, the Toshogu shrine, and the songbirds—which I could swear were singing in a different, perhaps Japanese, language—I might as well have been at home in the Tennessee mountains. Forests rose everywhere, lush and green except for the red maple leaves. We Tennesseans know maple leaves. We know how, at their peak of color, maple leaves are the most brilliant celebration of the change of season. These Japanese maples, with leaves tinier and brighter than our own, were peaking two weeks after we had made our annual pilgrimage to the Great Smoky Mountains to see the fall colors.

Morning mist lingered in the warming day, drifting, escaping up the valleys, allowing the landscape to suggest more than it revealed. The dry smell of autumn defied the lushness, promising afternoon views of the holy mountain Nantaisan that are not rivaled in any other season.

I felt at home, surrounded by the red maples; the pines and firs; their giant trees, cedars, like our hemlocks and poplars, so thick that a family of tourists joining hands could not spread their arms around them. Kegon Falls crashed over a cliff that dwarfs Abrams Falls. The Sacred Bridge over the Daiya River looked oddly like the swinging bridges over Little River. Other than the reassuring rumble of a stream over rocks, the most frequent noise was children squealing while families played and picnicked and shopped on Sunday in the small resort town.

We ate pan-fried mountain trout at the Kanaya Hotel, a haven for Westerners since a few years after 1853, the year Japan opened its doors to visitors for the first time in two hundred years. Following lunch, we walked slowly up the main stairway to the hotel's second story, reading framed letters and inspecting faded photographs inscribed before the turn of the century. British and American diplomats and other travelers from Saigon and Manila, from Singapore and Hong Kong, had all sailed to Tokyo and then traveled by wagon to Nikko to escape the great summer heat of Southeast Asia. It was the same kind of escape from heat and disease and mosquitoes that drove early American white settlers and the Indians before them from the Carolina shores to the safety of the cool Tennessee mountains.

Japan is three and a half times the size of Tennessee, but two-thirds of Japan are mountains and forests. On the remaining third live 120 million people—thirty times as many people as live in Tennessee. That leaves very little room for anything else, like playing golf. We were startled to see Japanese on the roofs of Tokyo buildings, waiting their turns to hit golf balls into huge nets. There is no space for driving ranges.

John Eisterhold, a University of Tennessee professor, remembers driving a dozen Japanese children along Interstate 40, the busiest highway in Tennessee. "They were taking photograph after photograph of open land," John remembers. "So I said, 'OK, why? There's nothing there.'"

"That's why," one replied. "There's nothing there."

"I feel the sky is not so wide in Tokyo," another child said.

Japan's equivalent of Interstate 40 is the three-hundred-mile Tomei Kosoku Doro, connecting Tokyo and Osaka, about as far apart as Crossville and Memphis. Eighty million Japanese live within twenty miles of the Tomei Kosoku Doro. That is about twenty times as many people as live in all of Tennessee.

Among the crowds and concrete canyons, the natural beauty of Japan is sometimes hard to isolate, but it is there. The Japanese enjoy the outdoors even more than we Tennesseans do. For many, it is life's goal to be in harmony with nature.

Japanese borrow from nature. In their houses, the window frames a view of the moon; the view of the mountain is part of the garden.

They find ways to fit into nature. God made no straight lines in either Tennessee or Japan. The streams, the mountains, the shadows, the coastlines of Japan—all are in continuous motion. Man made the straight lines. The only difference is that outside the cities of Japan, man's lines are arranged *within* the landscape instead of imposed upon it, as often happens when *we* build.

The Japanese never miss an opportunity to celebrate nature's wonders. All Japan slows in April when the cherry blossoms are full. In Tokyo the blossoms are said to be the most beautiful around the Emperor's palace, near the British Embassy. There the ground is covered with Japanese picnickers, reclining with sake and rice cakes, looking up through fragile flowers draped overhead like pink clouds. Tennesseans understand that. At about the same time each April, Knoxvillians pause for seventeen days to celebrate the dogwoods' bloom.

The Japanese are fascinated with Mt. Fuji, a volcano which is endlessly reproduced on plates, in paintings, and on pins. We understand that, too. Some days, Charles Krutch, the Knoxville artist, painted *only* Mt. LeConte. "The shadows are always changing. It is never the same," he explained.

The Japanese delight in combining natural phenomena: spring buds in the late snow or wild geese descending to a lake. Tennessee fishermen notice things like that, too: "When dogwoods bloom, the crappie run."

I always enjoy watching our Japanese friends discover in the Tennessee outdoors so many familiar things, like our state flower, the iris, which they venerate, and unexpected things, like the magnolia, which is not common in Japan.

For three years, I have paid $2.50 for a small desk calendar at my favorite woodblock print shop behind the Imperial Hotel in Tokyo. Each month of the 1986 calendar celebrates a different Japanese flower. For January it is the narcissus, whose fragile orange-yellow blooms are also the first sign of thawing in Tennessee (although usually it is February or even early March before they break through our snow). With March comes the violet, which waits until April to spread under Tennessee trees. But, in April, Japan's season catches ours: their azaleas burst forth when ours do, and in May purple and yellow iris proudly stand everywhere in gardens in both countries.

Poppies and roses take center stage in Japan in July, and scarlet sage spreads along their roadsides in August. The chrysanthemum is their October flower, as it is ours. Since our winter returns a few weeks before theirs, the brilliant display of scarlet maple leaves is strictly reserved for November. During December, their favorite flower is our most popular holiday flower, the poinsettia. It is not hard to see why Japanese, who are so close to nature, feel so at home in Tennessee.

When Nissan president Takashi Ishihara and Mrs. Ishihara visited Tennessee in 1983, Honey and I tried to think of the nicest thing we could do for them. On a warm, late-October day, the four of us drove with three other friends to Cades Cove, the meadow in the midst of the Smoky Mountains that Lady Bird Johnson puts first on her list of places "every American woman should see with her family." We spread a picnic lunch in the grass near a spring by some big hemlocks. Mile-high mountains surrounded us, lush and green except for red maples at the peak of their autumn color. We celebrated the change in season. And we hoped our Japanese friends felt as much at home in Cades Cove as we did the first time we saw Nikko.

◄ *Preceding pages, 30–31:* Rhododendron speckles Tennessee's Roan
Mountain. *32–33:* Azaleas
decorate the slopes of Mt. Nantai in
Nikko, Japan. Sharing the same
latitude, Japanese and Tennesseans
enjoy similar climates and
landscapes.

◀▲ Tennesseans would be just as at home at Lake Ashi near Hakone, *above,* as Japanese would feel at Indian Boundary Lake near Tellico, *left.*

◄▲ A water lily at Nashville's Cheekwood cultural center, *above.* *Left,* water is used to purify the mouths and hands of visitors to Sanzen'in Temple in Kyoto.

◀ *Preceding pages.* In a practice known as *omikuji,* Japanese purchase paper fortunes at temples and shrines. Should the fortune be unwelcome, it is tied to a tree in the hope that it will not come true.

◀▲ *Left,* a small waterfall at Nikko National Park, one of Japan's most popular recreation sites and an important pilgrimage center. Numerous Buddhist temples and Shinto shrines share the rugged terrain with volcanos, lakes, falls, and giant cryptomeria trees. *Above,* Roaring Fork Creek in the Smokies.

41

▲ Brilliant autumn leaves offset the lush green of a moss garden at Nikko.

▲ Autumn in Tennessee — a traditional white picket fence snags a falling leaf in Knoxville.

▼ A traditional farm residence, or *minka*, in Takayama. It is in the *gassho* style, a name derived from the steep roofs, resembling hands held in an attitude of prayer (*gassho*).

◀ Much like a Tennessee mountain cabin, this Kyoto farmhouse blends gracefully with the surrounding hills.

▲ John Oliver's traditional log cabin and split-rail fence, in Cades Cove — a Tennessee-style *minka*.

▲ ▶ A scarecrow guards the harvest in a Japanese rice field, *above. Right,* the harvest in Cades Cove. Strong agricultural traditions are a common thread in the lives of Japanese and Tennesseans.

▲ A typical rural Methodist church, this one at Wildwood, in Blount County.

▲ A Buddhist priest feeds a pool of
carp – which the Japanese consider
to be a symbol of strength and

▲ The family cemetery at the
Hermitage, the Nashville home
of President Andrew Jackson.

◀ *Preceding pages, 52–53:* The
garden at the tomb of Ikkyu,
a 15th-century Zen monk.
54–55: Beautiful in its simplicity —
a church, a cemetery, the heavens
above. This is Henry's Crossroads
Methodist Church in Kodak,
Sevier County.

▼ The moon rises over an Amish farmhouse in Lawrence County.

▲ *Top,* a mountain farm near Fukuoka, Kyushu. *Above,* traditional roof styles at the Daitokuji Temple, Kyoto.

▲ A waterwheel at the Matsuo Shrine.

◀▲ Nature recreated: *left,* a balustrade frames the splendid garden at Cheekwood; *above,* a glimpse of the mossy ponds of the Saihoji Temple garden in Kyoto, created in 1339.

◀ ▲ *Left,* a classic Zen moss-and-
gravel garden at the Daitokuji
Temple in Kyoto. In sharp contrast
is the colorful tulip garden in
Nashville's Centennial Park, *above.*

◀▲ Flowers in bloom: *left*, the "Cherry Manor" in Franklin, Tennessee; *above*, azalea blossoms at the Nezu Shrine, Japan.

◀▲ The beloved iris is indigenous
to Japan, where it can be found
growing wild in fields and wooded
slopes. This popular flower has
been cultivated for centuries, and
several varieties were first intro-
duced to Europe and America in
the 1800s. Tennesseans also appreciate the iris: it is the official state
flower. *Left,* irises at Umenomiya
Shrine in Kyoto. *Above,* the iris
garden kept by Rachel Jackson
at the Hermitage.

◂ ▴ *Left,* iris gardens are common throughout Japan. *Above,* Malcolm Flatt, the gardener at the Hermitage, admires the irises in Rachel Jackson's garden.

69

2

The Match Game: Customs and Lifestyles

Tennesseans who visit Japan and Japanese who come to Tennessee have the same startling experience—first they are struck by how different everything is and then they begin to discover things that are alike.

City dwellers in Japan are already used to many things that are typically "American." In Tokyo, a McDonald's is not hard to find, teenagers in Yoyogi Park dance to American rock music from the 1950s—Jerry Lee Lewis is one of their favorites—and there is a Jack Daniel's Club that would make the good ol' boys from Lynchburg feel right at home.

When Honey and I stay in Tokyo, we run in the early morning around the Imperial Palace. Along our four-mile route, everything we see to the right seems American: eight-lane streets, new office buildings, modern hotels, English-language billboards touting Coca-Cola. To the left is old Japan, the walls and moats and gardens and lawns of the

Imperial Palace, built in the seventeenth century for Japan's most powerful shogun, Tokugawa Ieyasu. Since 1868, this has been the sanctuary for Japan's emperor.

On clear days, we can see the snow of Mt. Fuji. This causes the same excitement in Tokyo that East Tennesseans feel when autumn clears the haze that usually hides Mt. LeConte. In April, we notice familiar trees and plants everywhere along the sidewalks: pines, oaks, dogwoods, poplars, and bursting azaleas. In August, swans sit by the willows and katydids sing, drowning out the noise of traffic.

At one point in our run the sidewalk makes a long rise, narrows, and levels off. I always pause on this rise. Below, the palace grounds are spread out like a Japanese woodblock print, framed by a modern city. It is a blend of old and new, East and West.

On a visit to Japan in 1981, Honey had a belated Thanksgiving dinner with fifty Tennesseans who were learning to build trucks the Nissan way.

These Tennesseans had become celebrities, even oddities, living and working in towns outside Tokyo where there might be only a few dozen Americans among 200,000 Japanese. They swapped stories about the startling differences between Japan and Tennessee.

Japanese children had pointed at Basil Timoschuk, who is six-feet, eight-inches tall, and giggled when he stooped while riding a bus. A girl wiped her hand on Frank Johnson's arm to see if his blackness rubbed off. (It was the first time in ten years, her parents said, that they had seen a black person.) Other children pulled Larry Redmond's red hair, to see if it was real.

One story topped another. Claude Sawyer told about efficiency in the car plants, how one Japanese worker went for refreshments so the rest could sit together at breaks to talk about the cars they were building. No one had seen a Japanese car with a dent, or even a dirty one, and the plants themselves were so clean that visitors removed their shoes before entering, just as one does at a Japanese home.

No Tennessean had seen a gun in Japan. Everyone marveled at how children walked alone on busy city sidewalks, how single women were safe on the loneliest streets even after midnight.

There was wonderment at the casual Japanese attitude toward nudity: barebreasted women on billboards urging you to drive Toyotas and drink Coca-Cola and men and women taking hot baths together.

The Tennesseans feasted on turkey and dressing and told stories about Japanese food that topped all the others. Tom Collins had eaten several pieces of reddish meat with a half-frozen texture. It was raw horse. "I neighed for three weeks," he claimed. Honey told of the custom at parties of putting loaches (a fish resembling a small eel) in a glass pot of water over a flame. As the water warms, the loaches swim faster until, at the moment of boiling, the host drops a loaf of beancurd into the water. Thump, thump, thump, the loaches plunge into the curd to escape the heat. Triumphantly, the host pulls out the curd and slices the loaf into pieces amid excited yums from the guests.

Tennesseans, who like to slurp as well as anyone but who have been taught to feel guilty about it, admire the way the Japanese slurp their noodles, their soup, and their *ocha*, or green tea. In the noodle bars after work the slurping is so loud it is hard to hear conversation.

Tennesseans—who are proud of their own hospitality and courtesy—marvel at the politeness they find in Japan. Japanese strangers rode past their own train stops, left their places in long ticket lines, and even closed their shops to help lost Tennesseans. One taxi driver shoveled the walk clean of snow before taking a student to the Hirosaki train station. Our Japanese friends always stand in their doors waving good-bye until we are out of sight.

Examples of Japanese personal honesty are as frequent as those of Japanese politeness. You cannot lose anything in Japan. Richard DeMara left a $1,000 camera on the train to Osaka; a week later someone returned it in Kyushu, four hundred miles away. Overpay the storekeeper by fifteen cents and he will find you and return it. Throw away your old shoes in the hotel wastebasket—the desk clerk will give them back.

The sounds of Japan are sharp to a new visitor. Supermarket salesmen scream "irasshaimase" ("Welcome. Come on in.") at each new customer. The noise is like one hundred auctioneers shouting at once.

The street sounds are different. Trucks make pleasant noises when they turn a corner, and the garbage truck plays a melody when it arrives. Advertisers and politicians all use loudspeakers, occupying the silence created by the absence of honking auto horns.

At night the noises of the street are the noises of old Japan: in the summer, the clop-a-clop-a-clop of an old man's clogs on the cobbled street; in September, the tinkling bell and plaintive cry, "yaki-imo," of the baked sweet potato salesman; and, in the winter, the midnight thwacking of sticks, a traditional warning to take care with fire, used since the days when nearly all Tokyo homes were paper and wood and had a small open hearth for warmth. Sometimes after midnight the wail of a bamboo flute announces the noodle salesman, pushing his cart.

Japanese visitors to Tennessee also find some startling differences. The schoolgirls from Kanto who learn English at Lincoln Memorial University in Harrogate cannot believe "how much popcorn you eat and how big the Cokes are." Visiting students tell us that booing at sports is a singularly American sound. We are rowdier and noisier and sometimes late for appointments, which they never are. The sound of sirens on American streets and the availability of guns frighten them.

Our high schools are easier and our parents more lenient. There is more early dating here. If Japanese nudity surprises *us*, our public displays of affection embarrass *them*. There is no public hugging and kissing, there are no big grins, loud laughs, or slaps on the back in Japan. (If there were a Buddhist Santa Claus, he wouldn't go "Ho, Ho, Ho!") Our habit of saying grace before meals in puzzling to Japanese, who are Buddhist and Shinto worshippers. American women are much more career-oriented than the Japanese women we've met, who have begun to attend business social engagements with their husbands only since our first trip to Tokyo in 1979.

The Japanese, even with their perfect manners, have discovered some polite gestures among us that they admire. They have no custom of saying hello to strangers or waving from a front porch at every passer-by. In Japan no one holds the door for anyone. And Tennessee men who offer their seats on a crowded bus to Japanese women attract stares of disbelief.

Then there is the most fun of all, the Japan-Tennessee match game: finding things in Japan that are different but somehow match things in Tennessee.

For example, during a first visit, everyone notices how different Japanese and Tennesseans look. But after a few days, you think instead about how much people in either place look the same. Living on islands that for one thousand years have never been invaded and which for years banned foreign visitors, the Japanese have become one of the world's most homogeneous populations. Many of us have lived in our same coves and valleys and small towns for seven generations. In both Japan and Tennessee there is the same homogeneity which causes people to grow independent, self-sufficient, and skeptical of strangers.

The match game seems to have no end.

The sounds of the Tokyo fish market are like the sounds of the cattle auction in Lebanon.

The thousand paper cranes strung as a prayer in a Kyoto temple remind me of bottle trees in Grand Junction—a custom that has roots in the African practice of placing pots over the limbs of dead trees so that evil spirits can't escape from the earth.

Mrs. Ryujo Hori, the dollmaker who is a Living National Treasure in Japan, must have much in common with Hancock County dollmakers.

Both the rural home in southern Japan and the country church in Cades Cove merge into rolling landscapes with the same grace.

Everyone at the Gion Festival, one of Japan's largest, would have a great time at Mule Day in Columbia and vice versa.

On an autumn day at Kitano Shrine, Japanese businessmen sit at lunch beneath the changing leaves. They look like the bench sitters on the court square in any small Tennessee town.

The samurai code of honor is not unlike the chivalry of English knights or the sense of honor that drove Andrew Jackson across our state lines for duels.

Then, some things in Japan and Tennessee are just the same: the woodlands in Nikko and the Sugarland Mountains in the Great Smokies, the sticky summer heat, the dogwood trees at the Imperial Palace and at Centennial Park in Nashville, and the azaleas at Lake Biwa and the rhododendron at Roan Mountain.

Looking for minnows on the Kamo River is the same as finding them on the Little Pigeon River near Sevierville. Fishermen on the Katsura River in Kyoto would feel at home on the Tennessee River near Chattanooga. A Tokyo flea market looks and sounds like a flea market in Nashville. Spring planters and tobacco harvesters in Kyushu and Williamson County do the same work at the same time of year.

Japanese Boy Scouts wear the same uniforms our boys do. Tokyo Little Leaguers lose with the same agony Morristown Little Leaguers do.

Similar environments affect people in similar ways, even on opposite sides of the world. Professor Garland Smith at the University of the South at Sewanee has even suggested that Japan and Tennessee have similarities because the United States occupied them both after a big war. Is that why Emperor Hirohito has a bust of Abraham Lincoln at his palace?

In our new enthusiasm for our Japanese friendships, we perhaps stretch comparisons a little too far. Let us remember the carp. We both have them. But in Tennessee, fishermen are trying to rid their streams of carp; and if they catch one of these mud-suckers, he is tossed away on the riverbank. In Japan, the carp enjoys an honored life, swimming in quiet pools in manicured gardens, awaiting each May's festival when his courage is celebrated as a fine example for Japanese boys.

The point is, we don't have to be alike to like and learn from each other. We can treasure our differences as we discover our similarities. There are two Tennessee walking horses in the Emperor's stables, and I have a wonderful Japanese woodblock-print calendar in my office. This doesn't mean we're the same—just that we're learning to appreciate the best of each other's cultures. That's a lot right there.

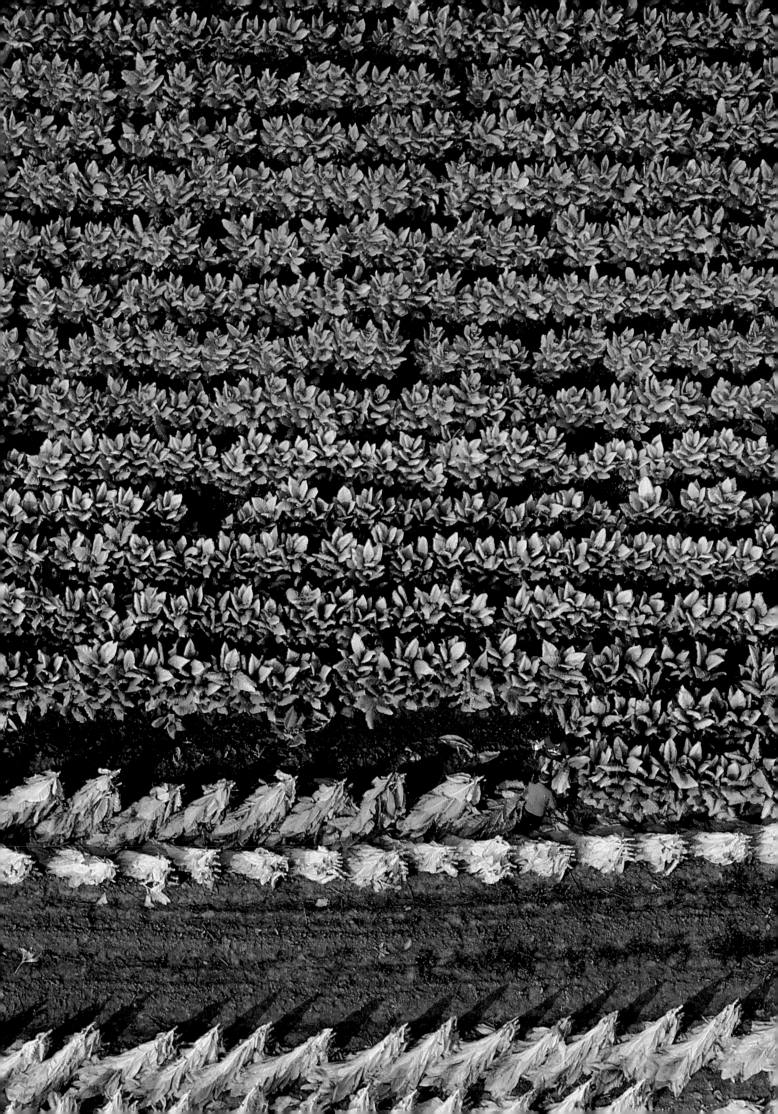

◄ *Preceding pages,* a tobacco harvest near Kumamoto, on the island of Kyushu. First cultivated in Nagasaki in 1605, tobacco has been a government monopoly in Japan since 1904.

▼ Much like the harvesters in Kumamoto, these Tennessee tobacco farmers in Williamson County put in a long day in the field.

▼ Shaded by wide-brimmed hats, women field hands harvest the lush green tobacco leaves. *Upper right,* dried and bundled tobacco is ready for processing.

▲ ▶ *Above,* a mule and horse
auction at Columbia, Tennessee.
Right, a tuna auction at Tokyo's
famous Tsukiji fish market.

◄ *Preceding pages.* A child rides a colorfully caparisoned steed at the Morioka Horse Festival, held every June. The procession ends at a shrine where the horses, long important to the area's farmers, are blessed by a priest.

◀▲ The same meticulous work,
a world apart. The quilters are,
left, Tiny Baker, 92 years old, in
Norris with a quilt her mother made
more than 150 years ago; and
Shizue Kadowaki, *above,* in Kyoto.

◄ Hands are the ultimate tool of the craftsman the world over, duplicating traditions passed down for generations. *Far left,* a basketmaker from Norris, Tennessee, weaves a seat for a straight-backed chair. *Left,* a Kyoto potter teases a perfect shape from clay.

◄▲ Dollmakers, East and West. *Above,* Toy Webb, a Hancock County artisan, has fashioned a miniature Tennessean in classic "good ol' boy" costume. *Left,* Ryujo Hori—designated a Living National Treasure by the Japanese government—exhibits her unique style of *kimekomi ningyo,* wooden dolls dressed in kimonos.

▲ ▶ A little sun, and a little time to enjoy it. *Above,* bench sitters at Kitano Shrine, Kyoto. *Right,* bench sitters at Belfast General Store, Lincoln County.

▶ *Following pages, 90:* Paper cranes at a Kyoto temple. Japanese custom holds that, if you fold a thousand paper cranes and string them up in a temple, you will speed the recovery of a sick loved one.
91: A bottle tree in Grand Junction, west Tennessee. The custom dates back, through black heritage, to an African practice of covering the ends of dead tree limbs with pots, to prevent evil spirits from escaping the earth.

▲ ▶ Backstage at the Grand
Kabuki Theater, an eight-year-old
actor, Kamejiro Ichikawa, is trans-
formed from boy to girl. Kabuki,
a lavish popular entertainment, has
been an all-male theatrical tradition
since 1652. *Right,* the actor is ready
for his role as Hitomaru, the young
daughter of Kagekiyo, played
by the boy's real father, Danjuro
Ichikawa.

◀ ▲ Without doubt the most colorful and extravagant theater in the world, Kabuki recently made its first appearance in Knoxville. The kneeling actor, *left*, is Tamasaburo, a world-famous *onnagata* (an actor who specializes in female roles). *Above,* the actor Ennosuke Ichikawa.

▲ ▶ The show goes on. *Above,*
Kabuki actor Ennosuke Ichikawa
backstage in his dressing room.
Right, Grandpa Jones onstage at the
Grand Ole Opry.

◀▲ Nashville, of course, is the home of country music, one of the many Western musical styles now popular in Japan, too. *Above,* Roy Acuff tunes up in his dressing room at the Grand Ole Opry. *Left,* Hank Snow performs in full regalia.

▶ *Right,* Lee Greenwood adds horns to the Nashville sound. He would no doubt enjoy the sight of the statue in Tokyo known as Man Playing Saxophone.

▲ In a fraction of the time it would take a Kabuki actor, country singing star Tammy Wynette gets made up for a show.

▶ ▶ *Right and facing page,* Minnie Pearl — wearing her trademark store-bought hat — continues to draw belly-laughs from the crowd.

▲ Japanese Gothic: a farm couple from the mountains of Kurume, near Kyushu.

▲ A caretaker watches out over
Cable Mill in Cades Cove.

▶ *Following pages, 104–105:* In
a timeless agrarian scene, Roy
Sherwood takes a breather at his
farm in Norris, Tennessee.
106–107: As upright as the bean
poles she holds, a woman smiles
with pride at her family's garden
near Kumamoto.

▲ As his ancestors have done for centuries, a rice farmer plants seedlings in Uji, near Kyoto. Despite rapid industrialization, agricultural traditions continue to exert a powerful influence on the Japanese character.

▶ Wade Caylor pauses in the morning light in Miller's Cove. Turning the soil by hand, he is close to the rhythms of the land and seasons—a trait shared by many Tennesseans even in this mechanized, modern age.

▼ Proudly showing their wares: strawberries at a Takayama farmers market, octopus at the Tsukiji fish market in Tokyo, and pumpkins sold out of Russell Stark's pick-up truck in Springfield.

▶ A Cumberland Plateau pumpkin farmer.

▲ ▶ Cornucopia! A fish and vegetable market in Kyoto, *above,* and a farmers market in Nashville, *right.*

▼▶ There's just no tidy way to eat watermelon, whether you do it in Tokyo, *below,* or in Chattanooga, *right.*

▲ ▶ The world-renowned Tennessee
Walking Horse. *Above,* Clay Harlin
exercises a horse at his ranch in
Franklin, the area from which two
of these fine animals, now part of
the Emperor's stables in Tokyo,
right, originated. They are used
in special ceremonies at the
Imperial Palace.

Left, a child ties a fortune to a gate of the Kameido Shrine in Tokyo, famous for its blooming wisteria vines in late April.
Below, Amish citizens in Lawrence County—a culture as exotic and distant to most Tennesseans as that of far-away Japan.

◄ *Preceding pages.* Coal miners in Japan and Tennessee. *123:* Each day these Japanese miners pass through a formal Japanese garden on their way to the bathhouse and a hot, steaming bath (*124–125*)— amenities of working life in Japan from which Americans could learn something.

▲ ▶ *Above*, a guitar player in Ueno Park in Tokyo has the introspective look of a blues picker. Banjo-playing Levi Collins, *right*, strums at home in his Caryville cabin.

126

▶ *Following pages.* Bart Suttles picks a tune at Wildwood Grocery, Blount County. Guitars, dulcimers, banjos, fiddles—Tennessee rings with self-taught musicians. Some have Opryland ambitions, most just enjoy a back-porch get-together.

▲ ▶ All the world loves a parade:
above, masked members of the
procession in the Grand Festival
of the Toshogu Shrine; *right*, the
Christmas Parade in Nashville.

▶ *Following pages.* Dressed in their own native finery, these girls show that loveliness knows no borders. *132:* A Tennessee youth at the Franklin Rodeo Days. *133:* A Japanese youth celebrating Children's Day at Arashiyama.

◀ *Preceding pages,* costumes from the past. *134:* A young woman takes part in a Civil War re-enactment at Carter House, Franklin. *135:* This woman portrays a member of the Emperor's Court in the annual Kyoto Textile Festival, celebrating traditional garments produced through the centuries by Kyoto craftspeople.

▲ ▶ Need a lift? *Above,* a streetcar conductor at the Chattanooga Choo-Choo. *Right,* a rickshaw operator at Kamakura.

▲ ▶ *Above,* the Miyako Odori, or Cherry Blossom Dance, at the Gion Kaburenjo Theater, Kyoto. *Right,* country-and-western dancers at Opryland in Nashville.

▶ *Following pages.* Opening ceremonies of a sumo tournament in
Tokyo. Sumo is the 2,000-year-old
national sport of Japan, combining
elaborate ritual and quick action.

◄ ▲ *Left,* Tennessee wrestling
champ Jerry Lawler. *Above,* a sumo
match is won when an opponent
is either knocked out of the ring
or forced to the ground within
the ring.

▼ ▶ *Below,* the good ol' boys at the Jack Daniel's distillery in Lynchburg, getting ready to ship casks to a bottler. Some of those bottles might just wind up at the Jack Daniel's Club in Tokyo, *right.*

▼ ▶ Scouts are much alike the world over. *Below*, these Tennessee Boy Scouts get a taste of Japan at the Japanese Garden in the Memphis Botanical Gardens. *Right*, Japanese Cub Scouts enjoy an outing on a Kyoto train.

3

Japan Comes to Tennessee

The story of Japan's manufacturing and marketing successes after the war has been called an "economic miracle." Today, Japan is helping to fuel an economic boom in Tennessee. The Japanese have brought new plants and new jobs to Tennesseans, and something more: friendships that are being forged at the political level, in business circles, on the shop floor, and in our communities.

I was elected governor in 1978, just in time to attend the ceremony announcing Sharp Corporation's decision to put its biggest U.S. manufacturing plant in Memphis. Before that day, I had not given a thought to the importance of Japan to Tennessee. But Japan was under pressure to make in the U.S. what it sold here, and other southeastern states were avidly courting Japanese industry. There were already signs of Japan's interest in Tennessee. Sumitomo Chemical had a joint venture with Monsanto in Mt. Pleasant, and Toshiba, the huge electronics firm, had put its largest U.S. plant in Lebanon, Tennessee, in 1978. Memphis—"America's Distribution Center," the place where every Federal Express package goes before it is delivered any place in the country—had become home to Nissan forklifts, the Mitsui Trading Company, and Toshiba Medical Systems. Tabuchi Electric was ready to follow Sharp into Tennessee—it wanted its transformers in Sharp's ovens—and announced a decision to settle in Jackson. And Tennessee was in the running for the biggest prize of all, the Nissan Motor Manufacturing Corporation. Nissan was searching for a site somewhere in the United States to put the largest Japanese overseas investment in history, a $300 million truck assembly plant.

We worked hard to persuade Nissan to come to Tennessee. In fact, our state development officials and I devoted almost all our energy on overseas job hunting to Japan. During my first twenty-four months as governor, I spent eight working weeks solely on Japan-Tennessee relations—three weeks in Japan, the rest with an endless stream of visiting Japanese.

Many of the visits were general in nature—by the Osaka Chamber of Commerce, or the Japanese newspapers, or members of the Diet. I noticed that while we talked, our visitors listened. While we worked, they watched. While we luxuriated in translation, they struggled to speak English. Dozens of books have sold millions of copies to unbelieving Americans who are astonished by Japan's success. It is no secret. "We learned what we know from American scholars and businessmen who came to Japan after the war to teach us and whom we have watched carefully in the United States," explains Kazuo Ishikure, president of the Bridgestone Tire U.S. headquarters and plant in LaVergne, Tennessee. "There is nothing Oriental or mysterious about it."

More and more of our visitors were coming from Nissan. First came the planners, then the engineers, then the policy makers, all requesting mountains of information, often the same information. Masahiko Zaitsu, from Nissan's Los Angeles office, was a guest at the Governor's Residence eleven times in 1979 and 1980. Our children began to think of him as some sort of Japanese uncle.

The negotiations were complex, frustrating, and interminable, but in October 1980 I finally got a call from Marvin Runyon, the ex-Ford executive who was hired to run the Nissan plant. "Lamar," he said, "we're coming to Tennessee."

My smile was a foot wide. It was the biggest news in our state in a long time. That afternoon, I went to the airport to welcome Runyon and Nissan president Takashi Ishihara. Zaitsu was there, too, wearing a big Tennessee T-shirt under his suitcoat.

Why Tennessee? There were hard-nosed business reasons. Tennessee is in the center of things—within five hundred miles of three-fourths of the U.S. population. This minimizes transportation costs. (That's why Federal Express is here, too.) We have low taxes and right-to-work laws. (Some Japanese firms in Tennessee have unions, some don't.) There were also less tangible reasons. We can't take credit for the fact that Tokyo and Nashville are on the same latitude, that the dogwoods bloom when the cherry blossoms do, or that the red maple leaves in Nikko and Cades Cove spread their brilliant color at about the same time; but if you are looking for a home away from home, it helps to be in a place that looks and feels like home.

There's another factor. I like to say that tomorrow's jobs are coming our way because Tennesseans still hold to yesterday's values. In this, we're a lot like the Japanese. Our workers believe in working, and in doing quality work. In 1984, Tennessee-made Nissan trucks had eleven percent fewer defects than those made in Japan. And, like the Japanese themselves, Tennesseans are famous for their hospitality and courtesy. We've worked hard to make our new Japanese friends feel at home here.

We're obviously doing something right. After we made business history with the Nissan decision, Matsushita moved to Knoxville in 1981, Bridgestone rescued a thousand workers by buying a failing Firestone plant in LaVergne in 1982, and in 1985 Komatsu selected a site in Chattanooga to make construction equipment.

Between 1980 and 1985, the number of Japanese companies in Tennessee more than doubled, from fourteen to thirty-two. The amount of Japanese investment in Tennessee jumped ten times, to about $1.2 billion. The number of Tennesseans directly employed at those Japanese enterprises grew from one thousand to nearly eight thousand; construction, purchases of parts and supplies, and the turnover of an annual $154 million in Japanese payrolls creates three to four times more jobs than that.

Japanese investment in the United States is growing today at an even more rapid pace because of congressional pressure to force the Japanese to produce here what they sell here. Nissan, for example, made an initial $300 million investment and hired 1,400 employees to build 69,000 trucks a year. Five years later, the investment had expanded to $745 million and there were 3,000 employees building 180,000 trucks and cars each year. It is likely that almost all the Nissan products sold in this country will one day be made in this country. Such expansion increases the likelihood that Nissan will buy more glass from the Ford plant in Nashville, more tires from Goodyear in Union City, more windshield wipers from Tridon in LaVergne, more injection motor parts from Kanto Seikei, which located in Lewisburg in 1983, more radiators from Calsonic and weatherstripping from CKR Industries and more from the twenty-four other Tennessee suppliers it now has.

Over the long run, Bridgestone could hire more Tennesseans than Nissan. In Japan, Bridgestone has forty-eight percent of the radial tire market; in the U.S., only three percent—for now. Industry analysts predict Komatsu, with its new U.S. home in Chattanooga, will join

Caterpillar as the most successful manufacturers of heavy equipment in this country during the next twenty years.

Nissan, Bridgestone, and Komatsu are a new base of manufacturing in Tennessee. They are the kind of money magnets we have not seen very often here, collecting billions of dollars from all over America and pouring most of it into payrolls, taxes, parts, and services within 250 miles of their plants.

These operations produce other benefits for Tennessee. When word spread that Tennessee had captured ten percent of Japanese investments in the United States, it established a national verdict: the painstaking Japanese, at least, had decided that Tennessee is an excellent place to make quality products at a lower cost. That helped to sell American plants on Tennessee, too. Many people think that General Motors put its Saturn plant in Spring Hill in 1985 because Nissan had done so well in the Tennessee environment. We were the envy of every other state because the $5 billion Saturn plant is the largest single business investment in U.S. history.

Most American corporate headquarters had overlooked Tennessee. Now *The Washington Post* describes Tennessee as the "new industrial wonderland of American industry." Would this have happened if the Japanese had not found us first?

Initially, there was plenty of opposition to the Japanese companies. When Nissan announced its decision to locate in Smyrna, Carl Montgomery, a retired Air Force colonel, demanded that the County Commission rename the access road to the plant "Pearl Harbor Boulevard." But four years later, Montgomery had his picture on the front page of the Smyrna newspaper as he nominated a Japanese executive from Nissan for local Rotary Club membership.

A rowdy union demonstration marred the groundbreaking ceremonies at the Smyrna plant, which was being built by both union and non-union workers. But the main effect was outrage on the part of embarrassed Tennesseans, who poured letters of support into the Nissan offices in Smyrna and Tokyo. Even members of the state AFL-CIO helped to repair the damage, and participated in our Japan Forum in 1982, designed to teach us all more about Japan.

It's true that the Nissan employees have shown no interest in wanting a union. The Bridgestone Tire Company, on the other hand, in effect bought the union when it bought the Firestone plant in LaVergne. In July 1985, Bridgestone president Ishikure announced that Lex McCarthy, who was selling shrubs in Lakeland, Florida, six hundred miles away and five years from his last job at Firestone, would be coming back to work, the last of the laid-off Firestone workers put back on the payroll under Bridgestone management. Mr. Ishikure praised United Rubber Workers Local 1055 for helping to locate the last few workers. And he praised the workers themselves, for improving quality and tripling production of the plant's radial truck tires in the two and a half years since Bridgestone had taken over.

We've worked to make the Japan-Tennessee connection a success. We've set up Saturday schools to help Japanese children keep up with mathematics and the Japanese language, and we've made sure their credits were properly recognized in our public schools.

The Japan Center at Middle Tennessee State University did dozens of small things to make life easier for Japanese newly arrived in Tennessee—introducing two wives of Japanese executives to Lewisburg storekeepers, helping one Japanese family find special training for a deaf child who had a special aptitude for art.

One Saturday, our family invited every Japanese family we could find in Tennessee to the Governor's Residence for a picnic on the grounds. We figured our new Japanese friends would have more fun in Tennessee if they knew other Japanese living there.

Every other year, Tennesseans join several hundred other southeastern businessmen in Tokyo in a two-day fall conference with senior Japanese business leaders. On alternate years, the Japanese come to one of the southern states for the conference. They particularly enjoy our spacious, uncrowded golf courses. And they are learning to enjoy southern ways. Norishige Hasegawa, president of Sumitomo Chemical, and Eishiro Saito, chairman of Nippon Steel, ask about Brenda Lee whenever I see them. The tiny redheaded singer with the big voice spends up to fifteen weeks a year performing in Japan. She sings in Japanese and always packs the house. She has been invaluable in making the Japanese feel at home in Tennessee.

Thousands of kind gestures have been exchanged as Japanese and Tennesseans become acquainted. One Japanese executive exchanged war stories with Bill Long, who was a Marine colonel before he became our economic development commissioner. The executive told Bill how his family was without food when he was fifteen and the war ended. American GIs gave them C-rations and sweet plums. It kept them from starving. Bill could not find C-rations in 1985, but there was a carton of sweet plums waiting for the Japanese executive when he boarded his plane for Tokyo.

The frequent visits, the gestures, the warmth—the friendships— have all helped to create an atmosphere that explains Masahiko Zaitsu's response to the *New York Times* reporter who asked why so many Japanese businesses have moved to Tennessee:

"When I come to Tennessee," said Zaitsu, "I feel at home."

◀ *Preceding pages.* The Nissan plant at Smyrna, Tennessee, a $300 million project — the largest Japanese overseas investment in history.

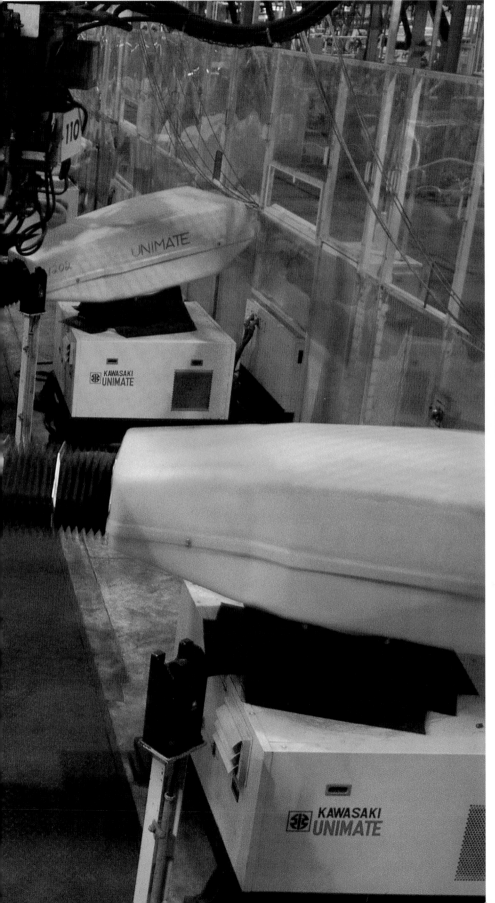

◀ ▲ *Left*, robot welders on an automated assembly line at Nissan — state-of-the-art manufacturing comes to rural Tennessee. *Top*, Japanese-style management: an employee production meeting. . *Above*, a Nissan employee on his break.

▲ ▶ Growing up together. *Above,*
two buddies at Bradley Elementary
School in Murfreesboro. Their
fathers are both Nissan employees.
Right, Bradley students put on
a music show.

◄▲ *Left*, the softball team of the Bridgestone tire plant in LaVergne. Japanese and Tennesseans share the same team spirit. *Above*, tires come off the assembly line.

► *Following pages*. Bridgestone employees H. Takigawa and Richard Thomas swap stories on their coffee break.

▲ ▶ Japanese enjoying Tennessee life. *Above,* Setsuko Kobayashi, the wife of a Bridgestone executive, in her Murfreesboro home with the homecoming quilt she designed. *Right,* Tosh Yamamoto and his family get Hank Snow's autograph backstage at the Grand Ole Opry.

◀▲ *Left*, workers at the Calsonic
Manufacturing Co. in Shelbyville.
Above, Calsonic employees Tim
Ochiai and Ed Butler have coffee
at Pope's Cafe on the Shelbyville
square.

◀ ▲ *Above,* Calsonic is one of the many Japanese-owned plants in Tennessee where Japanese and Tennesseans have learned to work together. *Left,* Yoshito Chikura and Bubby Naylor inspect a TV screen at the Toshiba plant in Lebanon, Tennessee.

▶ *Following pages.* Perhaps inspired by the Japanese interest in Tennessee, General Motors chose this site in Spring Hill for its $5 billion Saturn plant. The Japanese have been instrumental in spurring an economic boom in Tennessee.

4

A Bridge to the Sun

Watching the parade of travelers going back and forth across our new bridge to the Land of the Rising Sun has been the best front-porch rocking-chair pastime in Tennessee lately.

We've seen welders from Manchester leaving for Kyushu to learn how to make trucks the Japanese way; managers from Tokyo coming to LaVergne to learn how to deal with rubber workers the American way; NEC salesmen from Tokyo selling facsimile machines to Federal Express in Memphis; Grundy County producers shipping coal to Yokohama steel mills; Toshiba workers installing electrical equipment at ALCOA's Tennessee plant; Tennessee ash being shipped from Tullahoma to Japan for making baseball bats; the Grand Kabuki Theater coming to Knoxville; Brenda Lee going to Japan; soybean contracts passing from Humboldt to Yokohama; University of Tennessee students arriving at Hirosaki University to study Japanese and Kanto schoolgirls arriving at Lincoln Memorial University to study English; Saburo Tabuchi hurrying from Osaka to Jackson to see his four grandchildren.

All this activity has taken place in the middle of an ongoing debate over Japan–U.S. trade relations—a debate that exposes a sad lack of American understanding of Japan and its importance to us.

Here are a stack of major misconceptions:

They don't buy much from us. Wrong. Japan buys twenty percent of its imports from the United States. Japan is by far the largest overseas customer of the American farmer. U.S.–manufactured exports going to Japan create 750,000 jobs here.

They should buy as much from us as we buy from them. That would be hard to do. We are richer per capita than they are and there are twice as many of us.

We can do without Japanese products. We could, but we wouldn't like it. Who wants to send back his SONY Walkman or Nissan Maxima or Seiko watch? For a while, we would have had to give up all our video cassette recorders: every single one of them was made in Japan.

Import quotas and fees would show them a thing or two. We have proved that doesn't work. In 1980, President Carter put a twenty-five percent import tax on light pick-up trucks made in Japan. Then, Japanese manufacturers had about half the U.S. market. Today, they still have about half the U.S. market. So, for five years, Americans have paid higher prices for their pick-up trucks, American manufacturers have had less of the competition that would encourage lower costs and higher quality, and Japanese manufacturers, ironically, have been receiving the highest possible price and profit for their scarce trucks.

A more traditional American solution is what General Motors and the United Auto Workers are doing. With management cutting costs and with the UAW agreeing to wages based partly on sales, GM's new Saturn plant is ready to go head-to-head with the Japanese small cars on a level playing field in Tennessee. For GM and the UAW to get their own houses in order before complaining about the Japanese is good for the American consumer and good for America.

Japanese trade barriers are the reason Americans don't sell more goods in Japan. Partly true. Another reason is that we haven't tried as hard as we might. About half the Japan–U.S. trade deficit is in cars and trucks. Americans will buy 2.3 million Japanese cars in 1985, but the U.S. will export less than five thousand passenger cars to Japan. Each exported car has the steering wheel on the wrong side (for the Japanese), is too wide for most of the narrow Japanese streets, and, at least until recently, guzzled too much gasoline for a country where gasoline costs twice as much per gallon as it does in Tennessee.

Japan is responsible for the trade deficit. For too much of it, $37 billion of the $123 billion 1984 deficit. But we had a $20 billion trade deficit with Canada and a $10.4 billion deficit with Europe, too. Hobart Rowan in *The Washington Post* suggests bluntly that we complain more about the Japanese because they are of a different race than most of us.

The Japanese are buying up America. This is the most ridiculous charge of all. Despite the large amount of Japanese investment in Tennessee, the English, the Germans, and the Dutch each own about as much of us as the Japanese do. Altogether, foreign investment in Tennessee is about the same as GM's investment in the new Saturn Plant, $5 billion, only about five percent of our manufacturing base.

They are not really trying to reduce the trade deficit. Some are and some aren't. Generally speaking, Prime Minister Nakasone is and the agriculture interests, business lobbyists, and bureaucrats are not. Nakasone once told me how he literally demanded that the Japanese tobacco monopoly open to American products. The monopolists agreed to do it, "step by step." Why not try "stride by stride"? Nakasone asked.

But there is one widespread American attitude about trade with Japan that is correct and that Japan simply must do something about. *The Japanese must open their markets to us as much as ours are open to them, and they must do it soon.* If their markets are open to us, and we still can't compete, then we cannot complain. We could decide to close our markets, through a self-defeating protectionist system of import taxes, fees, tariffs, and quotas, but that would be an admission to the world that we cannot compete. "We are just too damn good to let that happen," President Reagan told me in the summer of 1985.

The Japanese interests that are fighting to maintain trade barriers must understand that Americans are upset not so much about the deficit, but about the unfairness of allowing Japanese companies to get rich romping in our playground—the richest market in the world—while we cannot romp around as freely in theirs. That is no basis upon which to build the most important two-country relationship in the world, bar none. It is certainly not the way friends treat one another.

Sometimes the talk of Japan is so noisy it is deafening: there are so many articles and statistics and facts and figures and explanations about why Japan has been so successful and why America has done such a poor job at catching up. In all the din, Japan begins to sound like our enemy again. The deluge of statistics leaves little time for talk of cherry blossoms and dogwoods, of sake and Jack Daniel's, of Buddhist temples and country churches, of feudal festivals and Civil War reenactments, of harvest festivals and kite flying.

For forty years, Americans and Japanese have compared statistics and discussed policy and jousted over trade. It's time we got to be friends, and recognized what that means.

Friends learn from one another. The Japanese learned manufacturing skills watching us in the 1950s. Our Nissan workers learned in the 1980s in Kyushu how the Japanese make trucks. There is much more, for both of us, to learn in that way.

Friends share and enjoy what each other has. McDonald's, Coke and Pepsi, Kentucky Fried Chicken, the latest western clothes, country music, and Jack Daniel's whiskey are nearly as common in Tokyo as they are in Memphis and Kingsport. We have learned to enjoy Matsushita video cassette recorders, Toshiba compact disc players, and Sharp solar calculators. A Japanese student at Lincoln Memorial University told me how much she enjoys shopping at Pigeon Forge in the Great Smoky Mountains. I told her that our favorite family restaurant in Nashville is Kobe Steakhouse, where we eat with chopsticks and watch a laughing Japanese chef toss food, knives, and sauces in every direction.

Friends help each other solve problems. The Japanese could learn a thing or two from us about how to care for an aging national population. We can learn from each other how to control social welfare spending and balance our national budgets. In education, they are loosening standards because of too much pressure; we are tightening standards because of too much laxity. We are moving, in opposite directions, toward each other. We have much to teach each other.

Friends need each other. We Americans need our Japanese friends in order to increase our chances for survival in this perilous world. The Japanese understand this better than we do. They live on four islands as close to the Soviet coast as Knoxville is to Nashville. Japan must have our help because the World War II settlement does not permit her to arm herself. "We are an aircraft carrier in the Pacific for the United States," Prime Minister Nakasone told U.S. senators in 1983. Later that year, he turned over to the Koreans—and to world public opinion—the "black box" recording that Japanese divers had recovered from the Korean 007 airliner shot down by the Soviets. The Soviets had threatened to interfere with valuable Japanese fishing treaties if the Prime Minister released the box. He did it anyway.

Gwen Harold, a Tennessean, and Hendenari (Terry) Terasaki, a Japanese diplomat, were married in 1931, against almost everyone's advice. The Japanese ambassador in whose embassy the couple met bluntly warned that their two countries might soon go to war.

"But we were in love," Gwen said, "two scared young people in love, and we honestly hoped our love would help to build a rainbow of peace across the Pacific."

Gwen told me what happened, on a visit I made to her Johnson City home in 1984. It was a visit I had looked forward to ever since I

176

had read her book, *Bridge to the Sun,* in one sitting.

After Pearl Harbor, Gwen chose to stay by Terry's side. They and their nine-year-old daughter Mariko were interned in Arkansas and West Virginia until 1942, when an exchange of diplomats from both sides took them to Tokyo.

The Terasakis became part of a neighborhood *tonarigume,* a twelve-home association organized for rationing purposes. "We would meet now and then and discuss what we had to do and where we would go if there was bombing. They never said 'enemy' in my presence. They always said 'adversary,' like it was a sporting event." When the firebombing began, millions of Tokyo residents buried their possessions and moved their families to the mountains for safety. The Terasakis went, too. "No one ever touched me, ever said an unkind word," Gwen said.

When the war ended, "like everyone else around us, we had lost everything and Terry was very ill. 'I know I can never be well again,' he told me. 'Take Mariko and return to your country. You understand. That will be best.'" So in August 1949, Gwen and Mariko, then seventeen, said good-bye to Terry on the dock at Yokohama and returned to Johnson City. Ten months later, Terry was dead.

In 1983, Japanese national television turned Gwen Terasaki's book into a movie, "Mariko," about Gwen's daughter. By popular demand, it was shown a second time. Mariko and her mother are now among Japan's better known and loved Americans.

"Why do you suppose the story touches the Japanese so?" I asked.

"It is not just for the Japanese," she replied. "It is a story for Americans, too. It's a love story. We were so different. But we had the same dream. We loved each other and we wanted to build a bridge of peace between the people of Japan and the United States."

When it was time to go, we talked briefly about the number of Japanese companies that had come to Tennessee and the number of Tennesseans who were traveling to Japan.

"Now, you know," Gwen Terasaki said sternly as I left, "you can help build that bridge, Governor."

The question fifty years ago, when the Terasakis were married, was whether there could ever be a bridge to the sun. Now, it exists, and Gwen must be proud of the remarkable role her home state is playing in answering today's questions: What travelers will cross that bridge? What will they do once they reach the other side? Will the bridge truly become a two-way street? And, will it be all statistics and business and policy, or will the travelers take time to enjoy the dogwoods and cherry blossoms and make friends along the way?

▲ Under Japanese and American
flags, families arrive for the Nissan
employees' family picnic in Smyrna.

▶ The Tennessee state flag flies
outside the Okura Hotel in Tokyo,
welcoming another delegation of
Tennesseans, now a familiar sight
in Japan.

◄ ▲ The Nissan baseball team from
Japan plays Vanderbilt University
in Nashville while on a summer
goodwill tour, another sign of
the growing human traffic on the
bridge between Japan and
Tennessee.

◄ A cowboy hat, a Nissan jacket: emblems of our growing bonds.

▲ The conference room of Kazuo Ishikure, president of the Bridgestone tire company in LaVergne. Japanese businesses in Tennessee are a boon to local suppliers and vendors.

▼ ▶ *Below and facing page.* It's
the young who are the quickest
to adapt to new environments
and make new friends, like
these students in Murfreesboro
and Nashville.

▶ *Following pages.* A barge makes its way past Lookout Mountain, Tennessee.

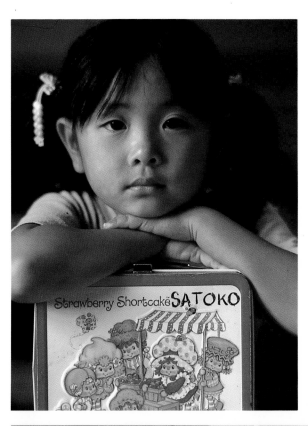

◀▲ Part of the increasingly busy
trade traffic between Tennessee and
Japan, Tennessee soybeans are
harvested for the Japanese market,
left. Above, a barge carries soybeans down the Mississippi, past
Memphis, for shipment to
Yokohama.

189

▲ ▶ *Above,* Japanese students at Bradley Elementary School often bring traditional sushi box lunches. *Right,* Bradley students—whether American or Japanese—take turns leading the class in the Pledge of Allegiance.

▶ *Following page,* the Tennessee state capitol building at Nashville. Here, the governor and his aides help to orchestrate the flourishing economic ties between Japan and Tennessee — which have brought to both Tennesseans and Japanese a growing respect for each other's cultures, and, the best treasure of all, many new friendships.